100 MODERN JAZZ LICKS FOR PIANO

Learn 100 Modern Jazz Piano Licks In The Style of 10 Legendary Players

NATHAN **HAYWARD**

FUNDAMENTAL**CHANGES**

100 Modern Jazz Licks For Piano

Learn 100 Modern Jazz Piano Licks In The Style of 10 Legendary Players

ISBN: 978-1-78933-177-6

Published by www.fundamental-changes.com

Copyright © 2019 Nathan Hayward

Edited by Tim Pettingale

The moral right of this author has been asserted.

All rights reserved. No part of this publication may be reproduced, stored in a retrieval system, or transmitted in any form or by any means, without the prior permission in writing from the publisher.

The publisher is not responsible for websites (or their content) that are not owned by the publisher.

www.fundamental-changes.com

Over 10,000 fans on Facebook: **FundamentalChangesInGuitar**

Instagram: **FundamentalChanges**

For over 350 Free Guitar Lessons with Videos Check Out

www.fundamental-changes.com

Cover Image Copyright: Shutterstock: Mikhail Bakunovich

Dedication

A huge thank you to my beautiful wife Rachel for giving me time and space to work, and to Chris Evans who gave many hours of his time and lent his considerable skill to help me record the licks.

Contents

Introduction	4
Get the Audio	5
1. Bud Powell	6
2. Oscar Peterson	11
3. Thelonious Monk	17
4. George Shearing	23
5. Bill Evans	29
6. McCoy Tyner	35
7. Herbie Hancock	41
8. Chick Corea	47
9. Keith Jarrett	53
10. Brad Mehldau	59
Conclusion	67

Introduction

There may be many reasons why you are reading this book. Maybe you're studying music at college, maybe your piano teacher recommended it, or maybe you're a piano teacher like me. Whatever the reason, approach this book with the same motivation that drew you to music in the first place: because you love it!

You can work through this book systematically or use it as a reference guide to dip in and out of. Whichever way you decide to use it, you'll get the most out of this book by listening to lots and lots of the music of each great pianist. You can't learn a language properly unless you hear it spoken.

I don't have space to offer an exhaustive analysis of each player's style, but hopefully you will gain plenty of useful insights into their playing which will add to your knowledge and inform the development of your own style.

Each pianist covered here developed their own personal style; they were innovators rather than imitators. In learning from them, it's important we don't become "copycats", but allow our own musical personality to emerge. That said, all of these legendary musicians were students of the music that went before them, so some evidence of the heroes who inspired them will be heard in their playing.

The licks in this book range from easy to quite difficult! My main concern was to capture the style of each player and to present the type of licks they would play, so you can gain an insight into how they construct their melodic ideas. When you find a lick that really catches your imagination, memorise it (ideally by both singing and playing it), learn it in all keys, and play it repeatedly until it becomes part of your vocabulary.

I hope the time you spend with this book will be both pleasurable and profitable, and that it adds to your appreciation and enthusiasm for these great modern jazz pianists.

Get the Audio

The audio files for this book are available to download for free from **www.fundamental-changes.com.** The link is in the top right-hand corner. Simply select this book title from the drop-down menu and follow the instructions to get the audio.

We recommend that you download the files directly to your computer, not to your tablet, and extract them there before adding them to your media library. You can then put them on your tablet, iPod or burn them to CD. On the download page there is a help PDF and we also provide technical support via the contact form.

For over 350 Free Guitar Lessons with Videos Check out:

www.fundamental-changes.com

Over 10,000 fans on Facebook: **FundamentalChangesInGuitar**

Instagram: **FundamentalChanges**

1. Bud Powell

Earl Rudolph "Bud" Powell was born in Harlem, New York, on September 27, 1926. His father was a "stride" pianist, his elder brother a trumpeter and his younger brother, Richie Powell, became the regular pianist with the ill-fated Clifford Brown quintet.

Keen for his son to have formal piano lessons, Bud's father enrolled him at age 5 with a teacher called Mr Rawlins. Mr Rawlins gave his young student a grounding in the classical repertoire for which Powell formed a great appreciation.

Formative for Powell was the music that was happening all around him. Pianists he heard on the radio – such as Fats Waller and James P Johnson – would often be playing in his neighbourhood. But his biggest hero was the great Art Tatum, whose influence can be clearly heard on Powell's solo piano recordings (check out his version of *Over the Rainbow*). Powell soon learned how to emulate the styles of his heroes and as an adolescent pianist became something of a curious addition to many of the "rent" parties (house parties where an admission fee was charged at the door to help pay the rent) that were regular occasions in Harlem at that time.

In the early 1940s, Powell became one of the circle of jazz musicians who frequented Minton's Playhouse. Here, a new style of modernist jazz known as "bebop" was being developed. Powell's associates included the greats of bebop: Charlie Parker, Dizzy Gillespie and Thelonious Monk to name a few. Monk, in particular, took a shine to the young Powell and became something of a mentor to him, even dedicating a tune to him, *In Walked Bud*, which has become a jazz standard. It's an interesting exercise to compare the playing of Monk and Powell, and hear Monk's influence. You can hear a certain amount of Tatum's playing in both.

Bebop improvisation requires not only a sophisticated understanding of harmony, but great technical facility, which Powell certainly had. He perfected an astonishingly clear and focused bebop vocabulary, proving that it could be done on the piano as well as on the horn. Powell was on the path to great things, but the fulfilment of his promise was hampered by addiction and mental health issues. His times of great creative productivity were punctuated by long spells in hospital.

Powell moved to Paris in 1959 and found a warm reception with European audiences. His time in Europe became the major inspiration behind the 1980's film *Round Midnight*. In 1964 Powell returned home to the USA and made some public appearances, but his behaviour was becoming erratic. He had contracted tuberculosis while in Europe and his health was deteriorating. Bud Powell died in 1966 at the age of 41.

Despite his difficulties, Powell left us with some remarkable recordings (check out his Blue Note recordings in particular). His contribution to jazz piano cannot be overstated. Along with Monk, he kept the piano at the vanguard of jazz innovation through the challenging bebop era. He was a composer as well as a master improviser and wrote standards such as *Bouncing with Bud* and *Tempus Fugit*. A study of Bud Powell's music is an essential for any aspiring jazz pianist.

Bud Powell's Style

The first five example licks are played over the common I vi ii V chord progression (in the key of Bb Major: Bbmaj7 – G7 – Cm7 – F7).

Example 1a uses a flat 9 note on the dominant chords – a staple of bebop vocabulary – an Ab note in bar 1 (b9 of G7) and a Gb in bar 2 (b9 of F7). Rhythmically, this is an almost unbroken line, except for the 1/8 note rest in bar 2 which creates a short, syncopated break. 1/16 notes and triplets sprinkled through the lick add some more rhythmic variety. Bebop phrases can sound like endless runs of 1/8 notes, but if you listen carefully to the great players you'll hear breaks, decorative turns and grace notes that create interest.

Example 1a

The next example begins with a typical bebop device. We're targeting a C note at the beginning of bar 2, which is set up at the end of bar 1 by playing notes either side of it. In bar 2, we're targeting an A note – the 3rd of the F7 chord in a similar way. Can you spot the b9 in bar 2?

Example 1b

This next idea illustrates how Powell might use the upper extensions of chords to form triadic patterns. For example, the last three notes of bar 1, played over the G7 chord are Eb, B and Ab. Respectively these are the b13, 3rd and b9 of G7, but can be viewed as a G# minor triad.

Similarly, the notes played over the Cm7 chord in bar 2 are G (5th), Bb (7th) and D (9th), which together form a G minor triad. Over the F7, an F# minor triad is implied. This is a bebop lesson from Powell on superimposing one tonality over another: G# minor over G7, G minor over Cm7, and F# minor over F7. Very cool!

Example 1c

Example 1d is a good example of how Powell used chromatic licks to connect chord tones. This device comes with a health warning! When using chromatic notes, you must have a clear idea of where you're heading – a target note on a specific beat. Random, directionless chromatics sound *awful,* whereas well-placed chromatic notes sound *awesome!* Notice that the line played over the F7 chord in bar 2 employs lots of altered tensions – the #9, b9 and b13 are all used to approach the target note of F which occurs at the beginning of bar 3.

Example 1d

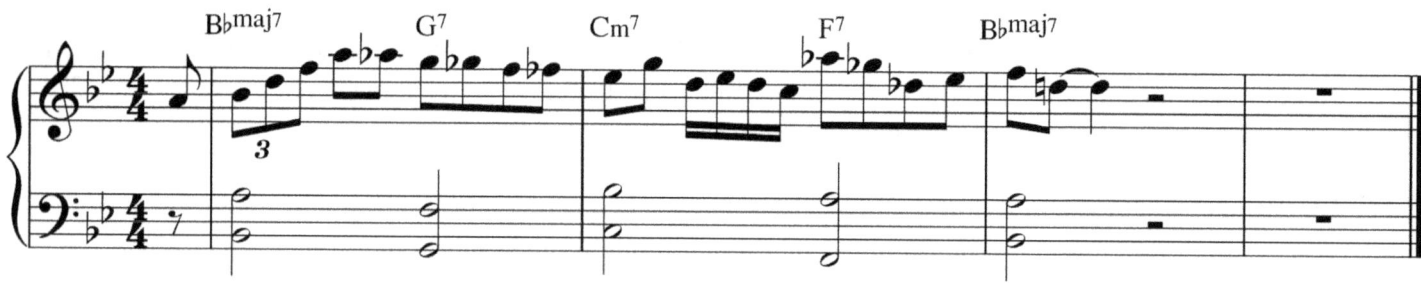

This next lick is pretty straight forward. The are no "exotic" notes, they are all diatonic to the key of Bb Major. The simple thing that makes this lick work is placing good target notes on strong beats. On beat 1 of bar 2, the Eb note is the 3rd of the Cm7 chord. On beat 3 the A note is the 3rd of F7. Again, the 3rd (D) is used for the Bbmaj7 chord. Played with a good rhythmic feel this lick will sound just as bebopy as the others.

Example 1e

For the next five licks we will change the progression to a ii V I sequence in F Major (Gm7 – C7 – Fmaj7).

The first example begins with a chromatic run beginning on A (9th of Gm7). Our target note is an F (7th of Gm7), landing on beat 3. Note that the interval between the notes A and F is a major third. Here is a top tip! If you begin a chromatic 1/8 note run on a strong beat and your target note is a major third away, you will automatically land on a strong beat. This is a sure-fire way of playing chromatic phrases that always work.

Example 1f

Example 1g begins with a 1/16th note figure to approach the root of the Gmin7 chord. Notice in this line that I play an F# note, rather than an F, even though the F is the 7th of Gmin7. When playing over minor seventh chords it often sounds better to sharpen the seventh in our melodic lines, even if the left hand is playing the natural 7th. In bar 2 over the C7 chord the line includes the popular bebop lick combination of the b9 and #9.

Example 1g

The next example features a cool trick that Powell would use. The target note of A would ideally land on beat 1 of bar 2, highlighting the 3rd of the F7 chord. Instead, it's played earlier on beat 3 of bar 1, anticipating the change by two beats. Lots of great jazz pianists do this.

Another bebop device featured here is the diminished shape used in the second half of bar 1. The notes A, Gb, Eb and C make up a diminished seventh arpeggio. Playing this shape a semitone higher than the root of a dominant chord (in this case Gbdim7 over F7) works beautifully. The Gb note acts as the b9 of F7 and the rest of the notes are shared by both chords.

Example 1h

In bar 2 of this lick, the line over the F7 chord uses the wonderful combination of the 13th (D) and b9 (F#). Adding an A note creates a D Major triad (D, F#, A). If you are improvising over a dominant 7th chord, you can always use the triad based on the 6th of the chord. (D major triad over F7; E major triad over G7 etc). It sounds great in the context of a ii V I progression.

Example 1i

For our final Bud Powell-style lick, the progression is altered slightly with the addition of a b5 substitution in bar 2. The tritone substitution is one of the most common in jazz – replacing one dominant chord with another whose root is a flat fifth interval apart. It is most commonly used on the V chord in a progression, as it has the same effect of pulling strongly towards the I chord.

The right hand notes in bar 1 strongly imply the Cmin7 harmony, and continue into the middle of bar 2, after the chord has changed. On beat 3, an A followed by a Gb note highlight the 5th and 7th of the Cb7 chord. Earlier, we played a line that anticipated the chord change; this time we are delaying it by two beats. It proves that harmonic boundaries can be very flexible in jazz, and pushing/pulling can produce some great results.

Example 1j

2. Oscar Peterson

Few jazz pianists have achieved the worldwide acclaim and popularity of Oscar Peterson. His music is instantly likable, full of joy and energy. It combines many elements: the infectious groove of the swing era, the simplicity of the blues, the virtuosity of Tatum, and just enough harmonic colour from the bebop palette to catch the ear.

Peterson was born on August 15, 1925, in Montreal, Quebec, into a relatively poor immigrant family. His father worked on the Canadian railway and was fiercely ambitious for his children, wanting them to earn better lives for themselves. Oscar received piano instruction from his older sister, Daisy (who eventually became a piano teacher) and his progress was regularly checked by his watchful father. Oscar learned and loved the classical repertoire, but also learned from the great Jazz and Boogie Woogie pianists. Peterson's ability made him precocious and noting that his son was getting big headed, his father bought him an Art Tatum record. The youth was so intimidated by Tatum's virtuosity that he didn't play the piano for the next two months!

Peterson soon made a name for himself in his native Canada. He appeared on Canadian radio many times and it was during a live broadcast of one of his trio gigs that he got his big break. Renowned jazz promotor Norman Granz was in Montreal and heard Peterson during a taxi journey to the airport. Granz ordered the taxi driver to take him to the place where Peterson was playing and a lifelong association between the two men began.

Peterson's entrance onto the US stage, and subsequently the world, happened in the most memorable way. Granz asked him to guest at Carnegie Hall with a collection of jazz greats including Dizzy Gillespie and Ella Fitzgerald. It was titled "Jazz at the Philharmonic" (JATP). Peterson was an immediate sensation and Granz added him to the bill as a regular.

Peterson formed his first trio while touring with JATP, consisting of Ray Brown on bass and Herb Ellis on guitar. The piano/bass/guitar ensemble spoke of Peterson's musical influences as Art Tatum had used the same configuration, as had Nat King Cole for his swinging trio. Peterson and his companions produced some incredibly intricate arrangements. Listen to *The Oscar Peterson Trio Stratford Shakespearean Festival* for the best of that band. In 1959 Ellis left the group and was replaced with drummer Ed Thigpen. This trio produced one of Peterson's most well-known albums, *Night Train*. It is quintessential Peterson and essential listening if you want to study his style.

For a jazz pianist, Peterson was incredibly successful, winning the annual *Downbeat* poll for best jazz pianist thirteen years in a row! He toured extensively and made a huge number of albums. He also wrote a book of jazz studies and etudes for budding pianists and even had his own TV show. His career spanned decades and he was still performing almost up until his death at the age of 82.

Oscar Peterson was one of jazz music's greatest ambassadors. He summed up the music that had gone before him and produced work that was dynamic, joyous and accessible. He raised the profile of jazz and his sound was an introduction for many, including myself, to the world of jazz.

Oscar Peterson's style

Example 2a begins with a descending flurry of triplets that spell a D diminished arpeggio over the G7 chord. This introduces an Ab note into the harmony to give it a bluesy flavour. Peterson was a very bluesy player and frequently used the notes of the blues scale. However, he used the blues like seasoning. In jazz, a sprinkle of the blues goes a long way, but it shouldn't be overdone. In this lick, the F blues scale (F, Ab, Bb, B, C, Eb, F) is combined with F Major Pentatonic (F, G, A, C, D, F). The personality of these two scales is so strong that they work over most standard chord sequences, even if the notes don't always fit the chords.

Example 2a

Example 2b features a typically Peterson short catchy idea that is turned into a motif. Interest is created by placing the motif on different beats in the bar. The displacement creates a pleasing rhythmic tension that is resolved by landing squarely on beat 1 of bar 3. This is the point at which the harmony resolves to chord I, so the line creates a strong impression of arriving home.

Example 2b

The next example begins with a descending line that approaches each chord tone of the G7 from a semitone below. After this, the line uses the blues/pentatonic scale combination again. This is characteristic of Peterson's style – some of his melodic lines were designed to *fit* the chord changes and others were simply played *over* the chord changes. His playing shows a deep understanding of harmony, combined with some stunning blues chops. Notice that in bar 2 there is a C note in the bass with a B note fleetingly jammed next to it. This kind of accented bass note – always played on the V chord and always on an off beat – was used habitually by Peterson.

Example 2c

Example 2d begins with a repeated figure on every beat. Like Example 2b, this type of line could be repeated over multiple bars to create even more tension. There is a "suggestion" of other chords in bar 2. On beats 3 and 4, the notes B and Bb resolve to an A at the start of bar 3. The notes hint at the chords G7, C7 and F, like a mini ii V I progression over the C bass note.

Example 2d

In the following example, a plain Gm7 arpeggio beginning on bar 1, beat 3 (an obvious thing to play over Gm7!) is kick started by the decorative notes that precede it. The approach notes leading to the G give the line a bebop flavour and act as a rhythmic springboard. Try playing the lick without this decoration and it doesn't quite sound the same. In bar 2, the chromatic run starting on Ab and landing on a C note on beat 3 is both bebop- and blues-like. It allows the lick to morph into the blues/pentatonic vocabulary for the ending. Peterson was influenced by bebop and you can hear it in his playing, but he is never far from the blues.

Example 2e

One of the best features of Peterson's music is the way he builds intensity through his solos. He seems to reach an incredibly high level of energy, only to break into the stratosphere on the next chorus! One way he achieves this is through his use of chords. Example 2f features chords played by both hands with the same rhythm. The melody note is played in octaves in the right hand to give it prominence.

The chords are not always completely tidy. For instance, the D7 that occurs fractionally after beat 4 in bar 3 has a G note in the right hand. Over a D7 chord this would normally clash with the F# contained in the chord, but here the right hand has been playing C octaves with a G note in the middle for a whole bar, so the fleeting discord is lost in forward momentum of the music. The tremolo in the right hand chord at the end of the lick is another typical Peterson device to build intensity.

Example 2f

Example 2g demonstrates a typical Peterson-esque bluesy figure repeated three times – each time an octave lower. On the third time, an A natural is introduced to give it a more "major" feel and add some variety. The line starts high on the piano and spans almost four octaves. This creates the powerful avalanche of notes that land with a thud on beat 1 of bar 3. This particular lick can be used over most standard chord sequences. Here it is played over the ii V I sequence, but try it over a blues or rhythm changes sequence and you'll hear that it works.

Example 2g

The final three licks are played over a I vi ii V progression in Bb Major (aka the rhythm changes, a la George Gershwin). In Example 2h some bebop influence is heard with the use of the #9 and b9 on the G7 chord in bar 1. The second half of the phrase reverts to the blues/pentatonic sound. It sounds cool to bring a phrase home with a blues lick, and Peterson did so frequently. The E natural to F movement on beat 2 of bar 2 is neatly harmonised in thirds. There are a few key places where the notes in the blues/pentatonic scale harmonise really well in thirds or sixths, and it's worth exploring this idea on your own.

Example 2h

Example 2i is a simple, single-note melodic idea repeated three times. As well as being catchy this lick has a very practical application. Repeating a catchy, predictable motif gives a band a rhythmic focal point to unite behind, which makes the time feel more stable. Peterson actually called these simple repeated riffs "stabilisers" – a trick he'd picked up from listening to Nat King Cole. Try it next time you're playing with a dodgy rhythm section!

Example 2i

As we have seen, Peterson wasn't just a blues machine but had a deep grasp of harmony. He would often throw in an "exotic" chord or melodic pattern to catch the listener by surprise. From beat 3 of bar 1, a series of arpeggios descend chromatically. For the chords G7, Cm7 and F7 the left hand plays only 'guide tones' (the 3rd and 7th of the chord), which means that the chords effectively descend chromatically. With just guide tones to outline the harmony, we can imagine the chord progression here to be G7, Gb7 (a tritone substitution for C7) and F7.

On the G7 chord, the right hand plays an A Major arpeggio. For Gb7 it's an Ab Major arpeggio, and on the F7 chord a G Major arpeggio. For each chord we play a major arpeggio with its root a whole step higher than the chord. The notes used to make up the right hand arpeggios are the 9th, #11th and the 13th of the chords below them. This trick of using the triad a whole step above the chord you're playing over works well over most major-type chords, be they major sevenths or dominant sevenths.

15

Example 2j

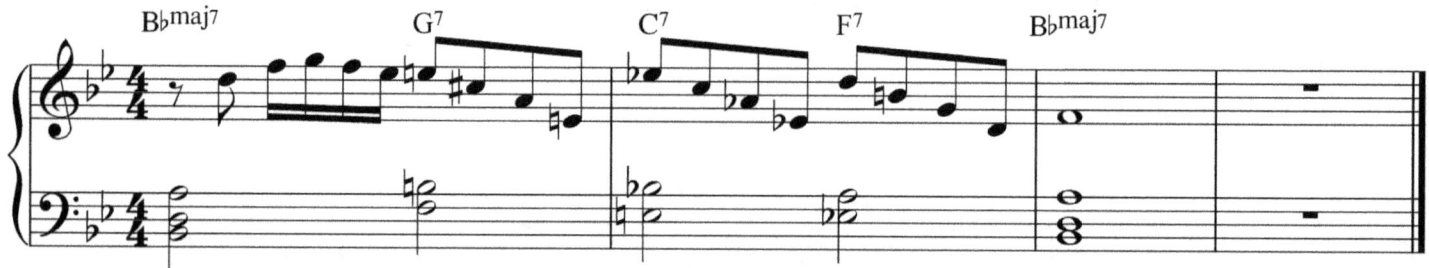

3. Thelonious Monk

On the 10th of October 1917 in Rocky Mount, North Carolina, one of the most distinctive personalities in the history of jazz was born: Thelonious Sphere Monk. His unusual name would suit his character.

Monk's family moved to Manhattan, New York in 1922. He showed an interest in the piano from a young age and was mostly self-taught. This may explain the individual approach he took to his music. He imbibed the styles of the great stride pianists and admired players like James P. Johnson (who lived in his neighbourhood) and Art Tatum.

In his teens he dropped out of school to embark on a musical career, touring as the organist with an evangelist. He eventually managed to secure the piano chair at a newly opened club called Minton's Playhouse (see the Bud Powell chapter). Here he honed his distinctive approach and was one of the inspirational musicians in the melting pot of ideas that crystallised into the bebop movement. The great saxophonist Colman Hawkins invited the unique young pianist to play in his quartet in 1944 which signalled Monk's first proper studio recording session.

Monk's style was full of deliberate but accidental sounding dissonances. The stride piano tradition and bebop harmony were put through the mangle of Monk's mind and the result was too puzzling for many of the jazz critics and listeners of the late 40s and early 50s. Though some believed in him, Monk's baffling style coupled with his seeming disinterest in self-promotion led to some lean periods for the pianist. Monk encountered a further set back to his career in 1951 when he refused to testify against his friend Bud Powell. He and Powell were in a car that was searched by the police and narcotics belonging to Powell were found. Monk had his "cabaret card" confiscated (unless you had one you could not legally perform in any venue that sold liquor in New York district).

In 1955 Monk moved over to Riverside records and released *Thelonious Monk plays Duke Ellington*. This album was meant to be a slightly more accessible cut and Monk was a long-standing admirer of Ellington's music in any case. For the uninitiated, this album is a good introduction to Monk's style. The next year, Monk recorded his landmark album *Brilliant Corners*. This album caused the critics to sit up and re-listen to Monk's work, triggering a resurgence of interest in his music.

An upward trend in Monk's fortunes continued. After regaining his cabaret card, he formed a quartet with John Coltrane on tenor saxophone for a six-month residency at the Five Spot Café. These gigs helped to establish Monk's reputation as a jazz genius and in 1964 he made the cover of Time Magazine. Monk continued to perform with his quartet, touring and making recordings.

Eccentric and mysterious, Monk's stage presence was unique. He would always wear some quirky headgear and while the band was playing, he would get up from the piano stool and spin around to the music. Towards the end of the 1970s his health deteriorated, and he withdrew from performing. He died of a stroke in 1982.

The name Thelonious Monk is now pretty much guaranteed to appear in any list of jazz greats. His compositions are still played extensively by jazz musicians around the globe, and his style has influenced not just pianists but all kinds of instrumentalists and composers.

Thelonious Monk's style

Examples 3a – 3d are played over the first four bars of the 12-bar blues sequence in Bb Major. Check out Monk's well-known compositions *Blue Monk* and *Straight No Chaser* which use this progression.

Example 3a begins with a bluesy interplay using minor and major thirds over the left-hand Bb7 chord. Notice the notes Ab and Bb jammed next to each other in the chord voicing. This is typical of Monk's angular sounding approach. In bar 2 the line rises to an A note, the #11 of the underlying Eb7 chord. The #11 was a favourite alteration of Monk's and gives a feeling of being far-removed from the harmony. Monk's use of the left hand is more interesting than many of his contemporaries because he uses it melodically, rhythmically and texturally, as well as just laying down the chords. The #11 is used again to end the lick.

Example 3a

Example 3b highlights Monk's use of rhythmic displacement and melodic development. It begins with a short motif. This phrase includes an A note, but the chord is Bb7 which contains an Ab. The left hand plays only one note to accompany, but the chosen note is Ab, as if to accentuate the mismatch of melody and harmony. Monk often chose to play one note instead of a whole chord (often the seventh on a dominant chord), which most of the time was just enough to suggest the harmony but meant that the left-hand accompaniment took on an almost counter-melody sound.

The motif is repeated but displaced to begin on beat 4 rather than beat 1. As the motif repeats twice more, each time the ending is changed, first harmonised in sixths, then thirds. The lick ends with a bass figure which lands on an E note, setting up the inevitable Eb chord which would come next in a 12-bar blues.

Example 3b

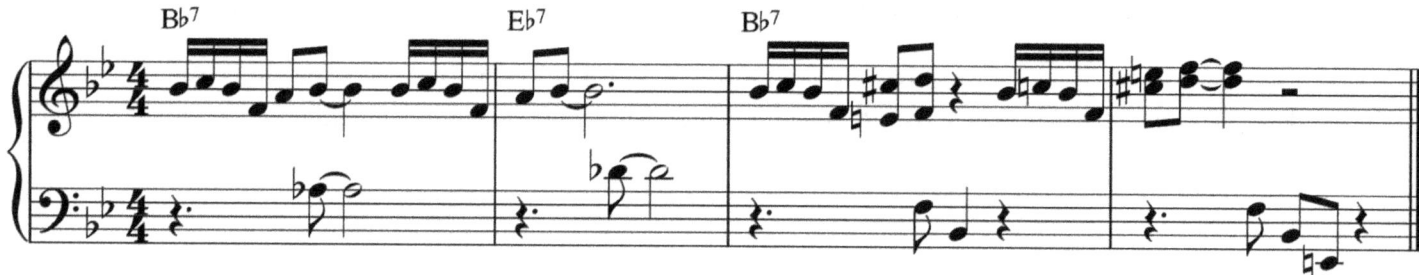

Monk loved to harmonise improvised melodies in sixths. In bar 1 of Example 3c the melody is mostly 1/8 notes harmonised in sixths. The 1/8 notes relax into 1/4 note triplets in bar 2 giving the last three notes of the phrase a more deliberate sound. The lick rounds off with a repeated motif, displaced the second time, as in the previous example. The motif is underpinned with low fifths in the left hand which accent the off-beat ending and give it powerful gravitas.

Example 3c

The next lick begins with a figure of ascending 1/16 notes. Most mortal pianists would use a scale or arpeggio here – patterns trained pianists have played countless times. Monk, on the other hand, plays something altogether more exciting: he identifies some of the more interesting notes of the harmony and uses them instead. Whether this is a result of his scant formal training or his original mind is a moot point, it's just great! A displaced motif and sixths both make an appearance to finish the lick in typical Monk style.

Example 3d

Example 3e appears to be fairly conventional at first glance, played over a ii V I chord sequence in the key of Bb Major. Monk could play things that were totally predictable, yet do so with his distinctive touch and rhythmic feel, to make it sound like *only he* could have played it. As so much of his style depends on feel (which cannot be effectively notated), it's important to listen carefully to the audio example.

Near the end of bar 1, the line has an F note (which we might expect to hear), but a dissonant E note is jammed right next to it. Is it a mistake or a purposeful discord? Does it matter?! Notice that for the F7 chord in bar 2, only one note is played for accompaniment, while the right hand plays with the major and minor third sound again (a preoccupation of blues musicians throughout history, and also of Monk).

Example 3e

Example 3f is a good illustration of how Monk's playing differed from his friend Bud Powell. Whereas a great bebopper like Powell would play lines of uninterrupted 1/8 notes with triplets and 1/16 notes thrown in for decoration, Monk's style was more broken up. Melodic motifs and the dramatic use of space were the tools of Monk's trade.

In the middle of bar 1, the sixth figure (landing on Eb and G) is left to ring into the middle of bar 2, creating a large gap that is broken only by the bass notes in the left hand. In bebop, one might expect to see a slick, linear passage towards the target note, but in the second half of bar 2 we see a run that appears to be heading for a D note (a logical choice – the 3rd of Bbmaj7), but which then jumps up a perfect 5th to land on the root note.

It's an unusual choice for several reasons. It's not what our ears expect; it creates a jagged rather than smooth line; and it creates dissonance between the Bb note in the right hand and the A note in the left hand. This is Monk's delightful world – always jolting us into the realm of the unexpected!

Example 3f

Example 3g again highlights how Monk uses space. The right hand only plays in bar 2, which has a 1/16 note descending whole tone scale run. This fast run sounds a bit like Art Tatum, but where Tatum would use mostly pentatonics, Monk opts for the more mysterious sounding whole tone approach – which works well over the V chord (F7) in a ii V I. Notice that the right hand doesn't play the expected Bb note to complete the run. Instead, the left hand plays the Bb in the bass and does the work of bringing the lick home.

Example 3g

Monk would sometimes emphasis certain notes by playing them as octaves, as at the beginning of Example 3h. The arpeggio that follows deposits us neatly on an A note at the beginning of bar 2. This A is part of the melodic line, but is played and held by the left hand and then becomes an accompanying note as the line continues. The motif that follows is a broken augmented triad that moves each three-note chord up a tone. This is typically Monkish and a more creative way to use the whole tone scale over the dominant chord. The lick finishes with a right hand octave, but the "crunch" of two notes a semitone apart leaves us with the unsettled feeling Monk no doubt desired.

Example 3h

The next example is played at a slower tempo. It begins with a jagged descending figure that includes repeated notes and wide intervals. In bar 1, the left hand pattern echoes Monk's stride piano influences. In bar 2, the right hand plays a figure harmonised in sixths, but with a C# note set against the D for dissonance. The chords are repeated machine-gun fashion, to make sure that no one misses the experience of their bone-jarring effect!

Example 3i

The final Monk-influenced lick is easier to play and includes some tricks we've already discussed. The right hand chords include both the major and minor third to jar against one another. At the end of bar 1, the melody notes are taken over by the left hand. If you watch a video of Monk playing you will often see his left hand becoming quite involved in the melodic lines. Here, the last note of the first melodic phrase (Bb) is held and forms part of the accompanying C7 chord. This idea of allowing a melody note to "melt" into the accompaniment produces a kind of sonic 3D effect.

Example 3j

4. George Shearing

George Shearing is responsible for one of the most famous and loved passages of jazz piano ever recorded. It's been on TV adverts, piped into shopping centres and has probably appeared on every "best of smooth jazz" compilation album in existence! You have probably heard it without realising that it's George Shearing on piano: Nat King Cole's *Let There Be Love*. Shearing's noodlings on this track are what make it so special and they are perhaps the most well-judged and effective improvised lines on record.

Shearing was born in Battersea, London, in 1919. His father was a coalman and his mother worked nights at a cleaning job. He was the youngest of their nine children and, unfortunately, born blind. Most families at that time had a piano in their front room, as did the Shearings, even though no one in the house played. At a very young age George would find his way over to the piano and pick out the tunes he heard on the radio. He attended Linden Lodge School for the blind where he received formal piano lessons and George's great talent was evident. It was obvious to his teacher that he was destined to be a jazz pianist.

After leaving school Shearing started playing piano at his local pub. He honed his skills in the Stride/Boogie Woogie style and soon graduated to more illustrious venues. His reputation grew and he soon became the number one jazz pianist in the UK. During the years of the Second World War he continued to perform and teamed up with the great French jazz violinist Stephane Grappelli.

By this time Shearing was a master of swing piano style, his mellow touch and technical assurance reminiscent of the great Teddy Wilson. He emigrated to America in 1947 and encountered the vanguard of jazz first hand. His style developed and absorbed new influences, including bebop. He had also perfected a way of harmonising melodies with block chords that became known as the "locked hands" technique. With both hands positioned to span an octave, he would create dense chord structures between the octave notes and this became a trademark of his style.

In 1949 he put together his most successful group – The George Shearing Quintet – comprising piano, bass, drums, guitar and vibraphone. The mellow tone of the guitar and the absence of horns gave the group a softer sounding edge. The instruments were also arranged around Shearing's locked hands style, with guitar and vibes often doubling up on the melody. They played mostly well-known tunes and took short solos. This recipe produced huge commercial success. Their version of the song *September in the Rain* sold over 900,000 copies and in 1952 one of Shearing's own compositions, *Lullaby of Birdland*, became a huge hit.

Shearing continued to tour with his quintet right into the 1970s before he decided to concentrate on smaller combos. He worked with many of the great singers of the period including Nat King Cole, Nancy Wilson, Peggy Lee and Mel Torme to name but a few. He kept working right up until 2004, eventually retiring after a fall. In 2007 he was knighted – a great honour for a man who had never forgotten his roots or lost his Englishness. In 2011, at the age of 91, Sir George Shearing died of heart failure.

Like Oscar Peterson, George Shearing helped to keep jazz in the public eye. His "locked hands" technique is now a standard part of the jazz pianist's toolkit and the "Shearing sound" is one of the unmistakable markers of the fifties era.

George Shearing's style

The first example of Shearing's style is less a lick and more an exercise. Any attempt at Shearing's style will inevitably include a generous quantity of "locked hands" technique, so to help you practice this approach (and me to explain it) Example 4a is a "locked hands" C Major scale.

Notice first that the scale is played in octaves – low voice in the left hand and upper voice in the right hand. Between the octave notes, three more notes are added that belong to the "source" chord we are expressing – in this instance a C6 chord. (Shearing tended to play major 6th chords rather than major 7th chords). As the scale ascends, if we encounter a note that does not belong to a C6 chord, a diminished 7th chord is played instead. The diminished 7th chords played on the scale tones D, F and B function like 7b9 chords.

Roughly speaking, this is how Shearing applied the technique to any piece of music. If the melody note was a chord tone, the rest of the chord was filled in between the octave voices. If the melody note was a passing note, rather than a chord tone, a diminished 7th chord was played. This is a general "rule of thumb" for locked hands technique. It can't always work perfectly due to the complexity of jazz music.

Practice the following example and see if you can apply it to some simple melodies.

Example 4a

Example 4b demonstrates the locked hands technique in the context of a ii V I in F Major. Listen to the audio example and I'm sure you'll hear Shearing's distinctive character. Diminished 7th chords are used on the passing notes. Notice that I've left the E note at the end of bar 1 un-harmonised. This is for ease of playing and because it's not the most important note to harmonise. There is no hard and fast rule to say that absolutely every note must be harmonised and it can sound better and help the fluency of the line if some notes are not.

Example 4b

Example 4c is another locked hands example. I'm labouring this technique because it takes time to get used to playing the dense chord voicings. In this example, I want to draw attention to the division of labour between the hands. The left hand tends to play the lower octave line and the right hand takes on all the other notes. This isn't a rule, by any means, but it does allow the left hand to add decorative notes that occur to the player when improvising – such as the grace notes in bar 2 of this example.

Example 4c

Now we break away from the locked hands technique to enjoy the more minimal side of Shearing's style. Shearing could play sparingly with incredible appropriateness and taste, as demonstrated on the aforementioned *Let There Be Love*. When playing with a string section – aware of the already full soundscape – he would barely use his left hand and stick mostly to right hand, single note phrases. In this lick there is nothing out of the ordinary in the harmony, just a few grace notes and a little syncopation to give it the reassuring informal feel of a jazz phrase.

Example 4d

Example 4e continues in a similar vein, though this lick has a more bluesy sound to it. When approaching this kind of phrase, which could have been played by any number of jazz pianists, the touch and feel become all important in capturing the Shearing-like sound. Shearing's touch was never harsh, but neither was it completely legato. It had a certain "poke" to it that helped achieve a very swinging sound. Listen to several of Shearing's recordings with strings and see if you can replicate his touch when playing examples 4d and 4e.

Example 4e

In Example 4f we see the tasteful right hand playing again, but this time the left hand has more work to do. Later in his career Shearing played more duo or solo gigs, so consequently he would play "four to the bar" chords to accompany his right hand and keep the rhythm going. The left hand chords fall on the 1/4 notes with an occasional bass note added between the beat. The left hand needs to be rock solid in tempo and rhythm for this to work.

Example 4f

Example 4g is a departure from the material we've explored thus far. Although Shearing's style is always easy on the ear for the listener, it can be technically challenging for the pianist. As well as mastering locked hands technique, anyone wanting to get to grips with Shearing's style must also contend with the long passages of 1/16 and 1/32 note runs he would launch into at the drop of a hat. Listen to the middle section of his famous *September in the Rain* recording for a great example of his. His technique is seamless. For this reason, practice Example 4g very slowly to begin with and increase the tempo gradually.

Example 4g

Example 4h contains another flurry of 1/16 and 1/32 notes. This lick shows how Shearing would draw on his bebop vocabulary for these quick passages. He was immersed in that world for a while and made some distinctively bebop-style recordings before his quintet hit the big time. Shearing's take on bop was more scalic/chromatic than most, as this lick highlights.

The overt bop style of his early American period eventually morphed into a smoother sound during his quintet years and beyond. Here we have some chromatism, but not many of the altered extensions (except the b13 on beat 4 of bar 2) indicative of the purist bebopper.

Example 4h

Next, we return to the locked hands style. At faster tempos, locked hands can be difficult as there is not sufficient time to play a chord on every note. In such cases we have to adapt. Here you'll see there are only five chords used in the lick, but it's enough to give the locked hands sound. A more sparse approach makes the technique do-able at a faster pace.

Notice in bar 1 that the left hand uses quick chromatic notes to create a "rolling down" effect. Rolling downwards or upwards, is characteristic of the locked hands style. The modern jazz pianist's left hand can get a little lazy, so locked hands technique can give it a much needed workout.

Example 4i

This final lick combines three of the four aspects of Shearing's style we have explored: a tasteful right hand line, four to the bar left hand chords, and locked hands technique. The only element missing is *Flight of the Bumblebee* style fast runs, you'll be relieved to hear. When you can drop any one of these techniques into your playing at will, you have mastered the Shearing sound.

In the first half of bar 2, notice the use of the b9 (Eb) over the D7 chord in combination with the natural 13th (B) in the melody. This chord is a typical choice when playing locked hands technique and its sound is evocative of the jazz of this period.

Example 4j

5. Bill Evans

Bill Evans is a towering figure in the history of jazz. His innovations opened up new dimensions to the sound of jazz piano and have become must-learn concepts for jazz pianists.

Born in 1929, William John Evans was raised in North Plainfield, New Jersey. His older brother, Harry, was the first to take piano lessons and grew up to become a jazz pianist and teacher. Soon Bill was taking piano lessons too, along with flute and violin. Evans studied piano at Southeastern Louisiana College and then composition at Mannes College of Music in New York. Like many of his predecessors, Evans was classically trained, but for him this was particularly significant. His training gave him a good technical grounding, but it also brought the influence of Western classical music into the heart of his style. Especially evident is the music of Ravel and Debussy.

Evans began to play in dance bands while he was still in high school and met and played with jazz guitarist Mundell Lowe. He listened to the music of Bud Powell and George Shearing, among others. Powell was particularly significant for Evans.

After acquiring some professional experience and serving for three years in the army, Evans began working in New York. He was heard by Jazz composer and theorist George Russell who booked him for a recording project. Evans began to make a name for himself and his first album for Riverside recordings was called *New Jazz Conceptions*. On this album you can hear some beautifully crafted bebop lines. In fact, the length of Evans' lines is commented on in the liner notes.

In early 1958, Evans was invited by Miles Davis to replace Red Garland in his sextet. Davis admired Evan's work and both men were interested in a modal approach to harmony which was new ground for jazz. In 1959, though he had left Miles' band by then, Evans was invited back to play on the album *Kind of Blue*. It has since become the bestselling jazz album of all time and it brought the modal approach into the mainstream of jazz thought.

In the same year as the *Kind of Blue* session, a bass player friend of Evans suggested they start a trio with drummer Paul Motian. The bass player was Scott LaFaro and the trio became one of the most influential jazz groups in history. LaFaro was a maestro bass player who could play his cumbersome instrument with the agility of a guitarist. He broke away from the traditional bassist's role of keeping time and playing mainly root notes. In addition to these elements, he was an equal melodic voice alongside the piano. The ensemble also allowed Paul Motian a freer role, underpinning the group's spontaneous ebb and flow using rhythmic displacement and musical space. On some recordings it sounds as though each person is soloing simultaneously – and essentially they were! But each musician never lost sight of what the others were doing and contributed to the overall sound.

The trio were together for two years before LaFaro was tragically killed in a road accident. Just two weeks prior to the incident they had recorded a gig at the Village Vanguard club in New York. These live recordings have become legendary and are the pinnacle of this trio's work; perhaps the pinnacle of all of Evan's trio recordings. Evans was grief stricken after LaFaro's death and didn't play for several months.

Evans returned to the piano, reforming his trio, as well as playing as a sideman. His style was now fully developed and he played pretty much the same way until his untimely death in 1980. His band employed various personnel through the sixties and seventies and proved to be a launch pad for the career of many great bass players and drummers including Gary Peacock, Eddie Gomez, Jack DeJohnette and Marc Johnson. Evans revolutionised the sound of jazz piano with his innovation in the areas of chord voicings and instrumental roles in the trio.

Bill Evan's style

In our first lick we see something of the bebop influence on Evans. Bud Powell had a big effect on Evan's playing and you can hear this especially in his early recordings. As Evans style developed, he kept something of the bebop vocabulary but gave his lines and phrases a more elegant shape.

In Example 5a an F target note on beat two-and-a-half is approached by notes either side of it, Bud Powell style. Bill's example is a little more elegant and lands on the F just before beat three anticipating the strong beat and creating pleasing a half beat break in the phrase. Over the G7 chord in bar 2 the bebop #9 and b9 notes are used, but harmonised Evans-style in thirds. This phrase is not so much about the 1/8 note run, but the varied note lengths and phrasing that enhance its melodic quality.

Example 5a

The next example is our first lick in 3/4 time. Evans often chose to play pieces in 3/4 and sometimes switched between 4/4 and 3/4 mid-song. We start with an A minor broken triad pattern in the right hand. The notes of the A minor triad (A, C and E) are the 5th, 7th and 9th of the underlying Dm7 chord. Evans often used the upper extensions of a chord to construct different arpeggio shapes. This technique could have been refined during his exploration of modal music – finding different sonorities to play over a static chord for an extended period. In bar 2 this same pattern is lowered to fit over the G7 chord.

Example 5b

Example 5c uses arpeggiated patterns similar to the previous lick, but this time they are four-note chord shapes rather than triads. Again, you can see one tonality superimposed over another. First, an Ebmaj7 shape is used over the Cm7 chord, then Dm7 over the F7 chord. In the second half of bar 2 a Bbmaj7 shape is played to anticipate the arrival of that chord in bar 3.

The motif is played a note lower each time and rhythmically displaced (another trick Evans enjoyed). Notice too that the left hand chords "shadow" the right hand rhythm, almost note for note. This left hand shadowing is *very* Evans!

Example 5c

Similar four-note arpeggios are used in the next example. This time the lick begins with a Gm7 shape over the Cm7 chord, switching to an Ebmaj7 shape which works over both Cm7 and F7 chords. Something of Evan's bebop heritage is heard is the second half of bar 2 with the use of the b9 (Gb) over the F7 chord. The arpeggios are grouped into four 1/8 notes, creating two-beat patterns. It creates the feeling of playing in 2/4 time, superimposed over the 3/4 time signature. It's another displacement device similar to that used in the previous example.

Example 5d

You may have noticed that so far, the left hand has not played any low bass notes. Evans tended to leave the low end to the bass player and concentrate on colouring the middle register with Ravel-like chords. Frequently he would omit the root note, which gave him an extra finger to play more colourful notes. In bar 1, the left hand is playing an Ebmaj7 shape, even though the chord is Cm7. The C root note has been omitted and the cool sounding 9th (D) has been added. When combined with the bassist playing the C root note, the effect achieved is a very hip voicing of Cm7.

Example 5e

One of the great advantages of using arpeggios is that you can harmonize them easily, which Evans did often. In bar 2 of Example 5f, the right hand notes are harmonised in thirds. Quite a few altered extensions occur in this bar, so it becomes easier to think of them as belonging to the altered scale. We are playing over an F7 chord, and the F Altered Scale contains the notes F, Gb, G#, A, B, C#, D# and F.

If you want a scale that gives you the bebop sound over the V chord in a ii V I sequence, the altered scale is it! It contains four of the commonly altered notes (b9, #9, b5, b13). Evans brings his elegant taste to bear by harmonising it in thirds.

Example 5f

Evans liked to play with chordal textures and rhythm. In the next lick, tension is built with a pattern that uses both hands equally. The left hand plays a chord on the first of each set of triplets and the right hand builds up arpeggio shapes.

In bar 2, the right hand is superimposing an Eb major triad (Eb, G, Bb) over the G7 chord. This highlights the b13, root and #9 of the chord respectively and creates a more "way out" sound. Octaves are added in the right hand at the end of bar 2 and the tension increases. Rhythmic patterns like this need to be played with rock solid timing, otherwise you're likely to throw the whole band off the pulse, not to mention yourself!

Example 5g

The next lick is an example of the "block chord" voicings used by Evans and others. It is written in the key of C Major for ease, but try it in other keys. In bar 1, the chord symbol is Dm7. You can think of this entire bar as being D Dorian (all the white notes from D to D) and move up and down the scale, harmonising the notes into chords. The first chord is a Dm7 voicing with the root and 5th in the left hand and 7th and 3rd in the right hand. This entire shape is moved up then down to form the melodic shape.

In bar 2, the chord symbol is G7, but we start with a surprising Fmaj7 shape. This is OK, because it is a fleeting part of a harmonised scale, which eventually leads to a lovely rootless version of Cmaj7 (the left hand playing the 3rd and 7th, and the right hand playing the 9th and 5th).

Example 5h

Example 5i is played over a minor ii V I in the key of C minor. The right hand part is harmonised in thirds throughout and consists mostly of 1/4 note triplets. Evans regularly used 1/4 triplets and "quadruplets" (four notes in the space of three 1/4 notes), especially when playing chords. The right hand chord in the final bar is a typical Evans voicing with no root. Here, the 9th (D) squeezed up against the 3rd (Eb) creates a sonorous semitone "crush" which is softened by the G note placed on the top of the shape.

Example 5i

The final Evans-style lick is played over the same changes. It begins by spelling out the notes of the Dmin7b5 chord beginning on the ninth. The ninth of a minor seven flat five is a really cool note! It has to be a natural 9, as the b9 doesn't work well on this chord, and yet the 9th (E) is outside the key of C minor. According to the harmony of the key, it should really be an Eb. This kind of sound (it works but it shouldn't work) is perfect in jazz music. It creates a slightly "outside" sound that tends to be quickly resolved.

It is resolved in the next bar, in fact, where an Eb major triad is played over the G7 chord. Notice also in this bar how the left hand plays a short descending chromatic figure to fill the gap left by the sustained right hand chord. Evans often used little movements like this, either in the inner voices of the chord or just underneath as here. The right hand triad is moved down a tone to a Db shape which works well over the G7 chord (a typical bebop b5 chord substitution idea). The lick ends on the same Evans C minor voicing as the previous lick.

Example 5j

6. McCoy Tyner

Like Bill Evans, McCoy Tyner developed a style that changed the sound of jazz piano, bringing a new level of intensity, power and assertiveness to the artform. Tyner will forever be associated with the John Coltrane Quartet, and it was in this intense, creative crucible that his sound was both refined and immortalised.

Tyner was born on December 11, 1938 in Philadelphia, Pennsylvania. He began piano studies quite late (aged 13) but had a very supportive mother. She let him practice on the piano she'd had installed in the beauty parlour she owned. He was also allowed to host informal jam sessions there. By his mid-teens Tyner was playing at many local jam sessions and gigs and becoming part of the fertile music scene in Philadelphia at that time. Notable contemporaries such as Lee Morgan, Bobby Timmons and John Coltrane were from Philadelphia and around to inspire the young pianist. Bud Powell, one of Tyner's heroes, moved to the neighbourhood and gave the youth some informal instruction.

John Coltrane took a special interest in the promising young pianist. While he was touring and making records with the great Miles Davis band, he kept Tyner in mind for a future project. Meanwhile, Tyner landed his first big job by winning the piano chair in Art Farmer and Benny Golson's "Jazztet" and played on the band's first album.

Tyner joined the Jazztet in 1960, but dropped everything that same year to accept an invitation to join the John Coltrane Quartet. Coltrane, with his legendary band of Tyner on piano, Jimmy Garrison on bass and Elvin Jones on drums, produced a sound that was dynamic, forceful and searching. The extraordinary sound of the band was due in no small part to McCoy Tyner's chord work. The material they played was often modal (staying on one chord for a long period of time), which allowed Tyner to experiment with powerful chords built from 4th intervals (quartal voicings), rather than traditional 3rds. In his right hand he would play shifting pentatonic patterns. Tyner created the wave of sound on which Coltrane's saxophone could sail with authority. The band became one of the greatest that jazz has ever seen.

Tyner was with the Coltrane group for five years, during which time they produced a series of extraordinary albums. He left in 1965 just as Coltrane was pushing into a more atonal approach. He embarked on a solo career which yielded much great music, not least the 1967 album *The Real McCoy* with Joe Henderson on tenor saxophone. Over the years Tyner has explored African music and also played with strings and big bands, but his quartal/pentatonic approach to improvisation developed during the Coltrane years is still very much his trademark sound.

McCoy Tyner is still a very successful jazz pianist today. He still tours and makes albums. Many jazz pianists have tried to emulate his style and almost every modern jazz pianist has been influenced by him to a lesser or greater degree.

McCoy Tyner's style

We begin this lick with a Tyner trademark. He often plays fifths in his left hand in the bass area of the piano – most often the root and 5th of the key chord. This serves two functions: first, it provides rhythmic punctuation to the right hand melodic lines, and second, it grounds the harmony. In the modal music that Tyner often plays it's common to create interesting sounds by moving motifs and chords around chromatically, but this can be disorientating for the listener. Grounding the harmony becomes very important, because it helps the listener remain connected with the tonal centre. After the low fifths we have some typical Tyner quartal chords. The right hand is exploring patterns in the D Mixolydian mode.

Example 6a

Example 6b begins with fifths in the bass followed by a quartal chord that repeats every beat and a half. The effect is a polyrhythmic carpet of sound. Over this, the right hand plays shapes drawn from both the D Major Pentatonic scale (D, E, F#, A, B) and C Major Pentatonic scale (C, D, E, G, A). If you're going to play modal jazz, knowing your pentatonic scales is essential!

Example 6b

Example 6c illustrates the typical explosion of sound so often heard in Tyner's playing. In this lick, the right hand tremolos D notes played as an octave, while the left hand thumps out bass fifths and then quartal harmonies in the midrange. It creates a dynamic wall of sound that sets up the melodic lines beautifully. The right hand notes used are drawn from the same pentatonic palette as before.

Notice that in none of the licks so far has the right hand phrase landed on a D, our tonal centre. Tyner will often avoid phrase endings that sound too obvious and the left hand fifths are always there to ground the harmony.

Example 6c

For the next lick, we move away from D Mixolydian and work with the C Dorian mode. This example begins in a similar vein to the previous lick, with low fifths and quartal voicings in the left hand and a tremolo in the right hand. This time we introduce another note into the tremolo – the fifth note of the scale (G) to create a "shimmering" sound.

In bar 2, a single note line emerges from this shimmering texture, using the C minor pentatonic scale (C, Eb, F, G, Bb, C). From bar 3 the notes descend in three-note units. Thinking in small groups of notes can make improvising easier and works particularly well with pentatonic scales.

Example 6d

Example 6e continues with a C Dorian tonality. From the scale tones (C, D, Eb, F, G, A, Bb, C) we can derive various pentatonic scales (C minor, G minor and D minor pentatonic are all contained within). In the last lick we used the obvious one – C minor pentatonic scale. This time we are using the G minor pentatonic scale (G, Bb, C, D, F, G). Shifting the focus to G minor over the Cm7 chord provides different colours for the musical palette. For instance, G minor pentatonic omits the note Eb (the 3rd of Cm7), but adds the more far out notes of D and F (9th and 11th respectively). The effect is to give the melodic lines a more open sound, slightly detached from conventional sounding minor harmony.

Example 6e

Example 6f illustrates how Tyner uses his right hand to build larger chord structures on top of his left hand quartal chords. Such two-handed chord voicings are common in modal music and Bill Evans used these exact voicings on Miles Davis' famous *So What*. The voicings consist of stacked 4ths with the addition of one 3rd placed between the two lower notes in the right hand.

The melodic line uses the third pentatonic scale contained within the C Dorian mode – D minor pentatonic (D, F, G, A, C, D). This pentatonic scale shares only two notes with a basic Cm7 chord (apart from the C). It does however contain some upper extensions: D (9th), F (11th) and A (13th).

Example 6f

So far we have seen how Tyner might employ scales that are not closely associated to the chord, to create a detached, unresolved sound. In the next example this "detachment" idea is taken a step further and we see a new chord progression superimposed onto the original harmony. Remember, we are discussing modal music which has long periods with only one chord. So, why not keep things interesting by suggesting other chords?

This approach can work really well as long as you resolve back to the original chord eventually. Example 6g uses the tried and tested approach of shifting up a semitone. Cm7 is our chord and the melody notes belong to the G minor pentatonic scale. In bar 3, the melodic line shift up to G# minor pentatonic and the left hand chord moves up a half step too, in support. The lick resolves by landing on a fifths chord (C and G) at the end of bar 4.

Example 6g

This idea is explored further in the next lick. The harmony modulates up almost immediately in bar 1. In bar 2 we take the chord up another tone to play a D# quartal chord. At this point we add the right hand. In bar 3 the chord rises another semitone and the right hand settles on an A major pentatonic pattern. The harmony drops away, down a semitone, then down another tone and the right hand line follows suit. Notice the use of fourths in the right hand line – this is typical Tyner. After experimenting with the different tonalities, the lick is grounded with left hand fifths at the end.

Example 6h

Example 6i is a longer lick. It is intended partly as an exercise in smoothly moving left hand quartal chords. It gives a good insight into how Tyner can go on crazy harmonic excursions while still holding strongly to the tonal centre.

The right hand plays a shimmering tremolo pattern throughout using the notes C, G and C, reminding us of the tonal centre. The left hand starts as previous licks, but soon shifts up a semitone, then a tone. Every two bars the left hand is grounded with those fifths, but the quartal chords continue to ascend. This creates great harmonic tension, but due to the grounding fifths and insistent right hand, we never lose sight of the core harmony.

Example 6i

For the final lick we return to a D minor tonality with a similar idea to the previous lick. Rather than a tremolo in the right hand we have a controlled 1/16th note figure using notes from D minor pentatonic. This motif loops over and over while the left hand explores harmonic jumps. The last quartal chord in bar 1 jumps up a minor 3rd, and then a tone in bar 2. There is a low fifth in bar 3 to ground proceedings briefly, which is followed by quartal chords descending in tones before the final fifths bring the lick home.

Example 6j

7. Herbie Hancock

Herbie Hancock has been a formidable presence in the jazz scene for over fifty years and during that time his work has spanned a wide spectrum of music. From being an integral part of the cutting edge Miles Davis Quintet in the 1960s, to a Top 10 chart hit in the eighties, from the avant-garde to the accessible and everything in between – Herbie has been there and done that. He is the consummate modern jazz pianist and pretty much defines the label.

Herbie Jeffrey Hancock was born in Chicago on April 12, 1940. He began piano lessons aged 7 and was something of a child prodigy. He absorbed and performed the classical repertoire which gave him both a technical grounding and an insight into the music that would influence him later in life. He then developed an interest in jazz and found that he could pick up complex harmonies by ear.

In his late teens he went to college at Grinnell in Iowa and double-majored in music and electrical engineering. He was already a proficient jazz pianist and was playing professional gigs as well as studying. He came to the attention of several jazz greats including Coleman Hawkins and Donald Byrd, being invited to play on the latter's *Free Form* album. His reputation grew and in 1962 he recorded his first album for Blue Note called *Takin' Off,* which comprised original tunes including the famous *Watermelon Man*.

Miles Davis became aware of the pianist and invited him to his house, along with young bassist Ron Carter and drummer Anthony Williams. This rhythm section became the core of the legendary Miles Davis Quintet in the mid-to-late sixties. They stretched the boundaries of jazz convention, playing with time, groove, harmony and form. Hancock himself continued to make successful albums for Blue Note throughout this period. Among them was *Maiden Voyage*. The title track and the final track of the album, *Dolphin Dance*, both became jazz standards. Another album, *Empyrean Isles*, contained the classic track *Cantaloupe Island*.

Hancock drew from many sources as his style developed. When he first began with Miles Davis he sounded a little like an amalgam of Wynton Kelly and Bill Evans (both previous pianists for Miles). He had the harmonic sophistication of Evans but the deep soulful swing feel of Kelly. He went on to draw from his classical training, adding Ravel- and Debussy-like textures to his music. He also explored Evans-like polyrhythms and pushed the harmonic limits further with Tyner-like quartal chords (though never sounding at all like McCoy Tyner).

In the late sixties Miles Davis began to experiment with electric instruments and rock and pop grooves. Herbie became enthralled with the new possibilities that were emerging and after his tenure with Miles ended, he made various recordings with electronic keyboard instruments. In 1973 he produced the landmark jazz funk album *Headhunters* which included a new and very different version of *Watermelon Man*, plus the classic funk track *Chameleon*.

Hancock continued his search for new sounds and grooves in the world of electronic music. He also continued playing acoustic piano, touring with his old friends Ron Carter and Anthony Williams, as well as recording and touring a piano duet with Chick Corea. In 1983 he had a huge commercial hit with the single *Rockit*.

Herbie Hancock continues to be an active voice in the world of music today. Lately he produces music that sees him in the more conventional jazz chair, but he is still questing for new sounds. He certainly deserves to be called a jazz legend and his style must be studied by any serious student of jazz piano.

Herbie Hancock's style

The first three Hancock-style licks are all played over three bars of Fm7. The first one is derived from Herbie's funkier music of the early '60s. The sound suggests a strong blues element, but in fact the harmonic language comes entirely from the F Dorian mode (F, G, Ab, Bb, C, D, Eb).

We begin with a rapid chromatic "slide" to the note D from the C below. It's this kind of inflection that gives the phrase its bluesy feel. The grace note on beat 3 of bar 1 serves the same purpose. On the last beat of bar 2, the left hand punctuates the lick by taking the chord up a semitone to F# minor, then down again in the next beat. The semitone shift is a well-known ploy in modal music.

Example 7a

The second lick begins with a long period of silence in the right hand, with the left hand providing harmony and rhythm with an Evans-like rootless Fm7 voicing. Just after beat 3 of bar 2, the right hand plays Evans-like arpeggios. An Eb major arpeggio shape is followed by Ab major arpeggio which is supported in the left hand with a C7 altered chord. The C7alt is added for flavour. Although the chart specifies four bars of Fm7, the pianist has the power to suggest other appropriate chords – in this instance a V chord that strongly wants to resolve to its I chord of Fm7.

On the first beat of bar 3, as the left hand chord resolves to Fm7, the right hand plays an "outside" E natural and enforces its surprising sound with an octave tremolo. This has the effect of "forcing" the underlying chord to become an FminMaj7. This tension is resolved by a chromatic approach to an F note from above, followed by a motif that winds down the lick to end on Ab. The overall effect is that of jazz wizardry thrown into a funky blues mix. The lick really belongs to the bebop heritage of jazz, but Herbie is a master of knowing exactly when and where to play ideas like this.

Example 7b

Like the previous lick, the next Hancock-style idea uses small arpeggiated figures. Here, broken chords are constructed on each ascending degree of the F Dorian mode. As the figure rises it creates excitement and tension which climaxes at the beginning of bar 3 with an octave tremolo on a Bb note (the 11th of Fmin7). Herbie seems fond of the minor 11 sound and the tremolo octaves are also very Herbie. An Abmaj7 arpeggio ends the phrase landing on a G (9th of Fm7).

Example 7c

The next three licks are played over a ii V I sequence in C Major (Dm7 – G7 – Cmaj7). Example 7d begins with a rootless Dmin7 chord, followed by a low fifth (D and A) in the left hand. Hancock uses the fifths differently to McCoy Tyner. It provides some harmonic support, but it's main purpose is to give a rhythmic "bump" which the right hand melody springs off. The melodic line is from the bebop canon and dances around the desired target note of D.

The lick begins with the D Dorian scale, but quickly morphs into the G Altered scale in anticipation of the coming G7. Hancock is a master of fusing together two scales to form one long line. At the end of bar 2, octaves are used again to reach a climax. The lick ends with a bluesy inflection over the Cmaj7 chord.

Example 7d

Example 7e is all about capturing the incredible *feel* of Herbie Hancock. You can hear a little of the Wynton Kelly influence in this respect, but the chord voicings come straight from Bill Evans' influence on Hancock. In bar 1 we begin with a short phrase that is heading for a G note to anticipate the next chord. In bar 2, notice how the G7 chord is approached from a semitone above using rootless altered 7th chords, spread between the hands. The G7 chord is repeated twice, and the second time the two lower right hand voices (Bb and Eb – #9 and b13) move down a tone to Ab and Db (b9 and #11) to create more interest for the ear.

Example 7e

Herbie is a master of creating textures and building tension. In Example 7f we have an ascending arpeggiated pattern that seems to become airborne, floating above the harmony and pulse. The rhythmic effect is created by grouping 1/8 note triplets into fours, so that three groups are played in a four-beat bar. It gives the impression of floating away from the pulse while somehow staying in time.

The arpeggio pattern moves up a step for each four-note cycle. Over the Dm7 chord, the notes are from D Dorian. Over the G7, a series of superimposed arpeggios (Db major, Eb major and E major) highlight altered extensions of the chord. Over G7, the Eb major arpeggio comprises an Eb (b13), G and Bb (#9); the E major arpeggio comprises E (13th), G# (b9) and B (3rd). Over the Cmaj7 chord a D major arpeggio is superimposed, which includes an F# (the #11 of Cmaj7), followed by an E major arpeggio which includes a G# (suggesting that the underlying harmony is Cmaj7-augmented 5th). The lick ends with an octave tremolo on a D.

Example 7f

Examples 7g to 7i are played over a minor ii V I in C minor. In this first lick, the line played over Dm7b5 comes from the D Natural Minor scale with a b5 (D, E, F, G, Ab, Bb, C, D). The line responds to the chord change in bar 2 with an Eb major arpeggio. Played over a G7, an Eb major triad implies a G7#9b13 chord. The descending triplet figure in the second half of bar 2 rubs against the swing time and brings the lick down to land on the 11th of the Cm7 chord – a cool note to finish on and especially sonorous sounding if you give your minor chord a major 7th.

Example 7g

For Example 7h we return to an arpeggio idea that would not sound out of place in a piece by Debussy. The harmonic language used is similar to the previous lick, but the rhythmic device we discussed earlier has been applied – triplets grouped in fours. In bar 1, after an initial G note, the pattern is as E augmented arpeggio (E, G#/Ab, C). In bar 2, this morphs into an Eb major pattern over G7 as in the previous lick. Once again the lick ends on the hip sounding 11th to create a CminMaj7 sound.

Example 7h

Now we return to groovy *feel*-based playing, but still employing sophisticated minor ii V I harmonic ideas. The lick begins with a simple, confident statement using octaves on the note of G. Bar 2 makes use of altered extensions (#9, b9, #11) for a bebop sound, but uses octaves and grace notes to inject some emotional energy. We finish the right hand on a two-note chord consisting of G and C with a chromatic/bluesy slide up to the G.

45

Example 7i

[Musical notation: Medium swing, Dm7(b5) - G7 - Cm7]

The final Herbie-style lick is played over four bars of Cmin7 in quick 3/4 time. As a pianist, the world is your oyster when it comes to long stretches of the same chord. As seen previously, you can impose your own harmonies onto the blank modal canvas.

Here the left hand is playing a rootless C#min7 and the right hand line begins with a G# note. After the G#, as the left hand chord moves down to Cmin7, there is a descending chromatic passage not unlike the kind of thing Miles Davis played. The lick ends with wide fourths intervals that provide a contrast to the tight chromaticism that precedes them.

Example 7j

[Musical notation: Cm7 in 3/4 time]

8. Chick Corea

Chick Corea earns his place in this prestigious group for his ability to produce extremely high energy improvisations which are also endowed with elegance and poise. He owes much to the piano style of McCoy Tyner with his extensive use of quartal chord voicings and pentatonic melodic patterns, but also the apparently contradictory styles of Thelonious Monk and Bill Evans. Bud Powell and Horace Silver are also present and Corea's family heritage sparks a Spanish flourish.

Born in 1941, Chelsea, Massachusetts, Armando Anthony "Chick" Corea enjoyed a musical upbringing. Aged 4, his father (also Armando) – a trumpeter who led a trad jazz band – encouraged him to start playing the piano. Chick began lessons with pianist Salvatore Sullo who gave him a solid classical technique. Like Bill Evans and Herbie Hancock, he developed a love and respect for the great classical piano repertoire.

Corea began playing gigs while still at high school and was very influenced by the music of Bud Powell and Horace Silver. He moved to New York to study in college but soon dropped out and landed significant sideman roles in the bands of Mongo Santamaria, Blue Mitchell, Stan Getz and others. He began making a name for himself in the mid-sixties and recorded his first album in 1966 called, *Tones for Joan's Bones*. It wasn't until 1968 when he released his second album, *Now He Sings, Now He Sobs*, that the jazz world really sat up and listened. This album featured Chick on piano leading a trio with the double bass maestro Miroslav Vitous and the great drummer Roy Haynes. This stunning album must be listened to by every modern jazz piano student! The sheer vibrant energy of the trio is a joy to experience – the work of modern jazz geniuses, still brimming with youthfulness. In 1999 it was given the prestigious Grammy Hall of Fame Award.

The next few years were very significant for Chick Corea and for the direction of jazz music. He began playing with Miles Davis, first appearing on the album *Filles de Kilimanjaro* sharing the credits with Herbie Hancock. As Miles plunged headlong into his new electronic fusion world, Chick mostly played his electric piano (a Fender Rhodes). Corea also embraced the avant-garde with the group Circle, which comprised his Miles Davis alumni Dave Holland on bass and Jack DeJohnette on drums.

In 1972 Corea produced an album called *Return to Forever* and this spawned the band of the same name. The instrumentation was a mixture of electric and acoustic. The music was (loosely) a fusion of jazz, Latin American styles and rock. This band was rocket fuelled! Stanley Clarke, the bass player, said in an interview, "We turned up and started playing much faster!" Return to Forever's second album, *Light as a Feather*, featured a track written by Chick called *Spain*, which has become one of his best loved compositions and a jazz standard.

Chick Corea has been involved in many and various projects. He has made countless acoustic albums, including piano duets with Herbie Hancock, and trios/quartets with various personnel. He still makes electric music with Chick Corea's Elektric Band and the reformed version of Return to Forever. He also performs classical music and has written classical works for string quartets and a piano concerto!

At the age of 77, Corea is still performing at the very top level. His innovation, formidable technique and highly individual sound make him a jazz legend of the highest order.

Chick Corea's style

In the first lick the influence of McCoy Tyner can be heard in a typical Corea lick. There are quartal chords in the left hand and the use of pentatonic patterns in the right hand. Chick plays with more space though. There are no fifths here, with which Tyner punctuated his phrases and the entire first bar is empty. The chord at the beginning of bar 2 is used as a springboard for the line that follows.

The space at the beginning of the lick gives the impression of the right hand line emerging from nowhere. Harmonically, the landscape is C Dorian. The melodic line, which uses the notes of C minor pentatonic,-is shifted up a semitone into C# minor territory and finishes on a C#, which is left unresolved.

Example 8a

Example 8b, this time in D minor, starts in a similar way to the previous lick – an ascending minor pentatonic line against quartal chord voicings. In bar 3 there is a definite departure from Tyner style with a chromatic pattern that has a fleeting (slightly Spanish sounding) grace note at the start of each little motif. The left hand chords roughly follow the melodic shape. The mix of heavily chromatic passages with pentatonics and quartal shapes is typical of Corea.

Example 8b

For the next example we switch to a D7 vamp and the ideas come from the D Mixolydian mode. This is typical of something Corea might play over the first four bars of a modal-style blues. The quartal voicing of a Gm7 at the end anticipates the coming change to chord IV.

Notice the use of *staccato* articulation in this lick. How improvised phrases are articulated is a personal and often intuitive affair amongst jazz pianists. Corea is more intentional than his predecessors and switches between liquid legato lines and dramatic staccato as he deems the moment demands. His use of staccato in particular is something unique to his sound and may stem from his classical training. The lick ends with an ascending G minor pentatonic run the leads into the climactic chord.

Example 8c

Next we explore how Corea might tackle a ii V I sequence in the key of C Major. Here we have a variation on the bebop concept of playing around a target note before landing on it. The note in question is a Db at the beginning of bar 2, which can be seen as the #11 of G7. Bar 1 contains a crazy, slightly random sounding chromatic passage that gravitates towards the target note.

Bar 2 has an ascending line that "settles into" G Major Pentatonic, but containing an Ab note instead of A natural. The Ab is a "bebop" note – the b9 of G7. The use of bebop devices reveals something of Corea's musical heritage, while the chromaticism and pentatonics show his understanding of the evolution of jazz piano.

Example 8d

Example 8e is played over another ii V I sequence, this time in Eb Major. Though Corea has made a lot of modal and fusion recordings in his time, he often returns to the standard jazz repertoire. In this lick you can see his staccato approach surface again at the beginning of the phrase. In bar 2 the influence of Monk on Corea emerges as the line almost "slides" up and down the Bb whole tone scale. The scale changes to Eb Major for bar 3.

Example 8e

Example 8f is played over the same ii V I sequence and opens in dramatic fashion with a left hand chord a semitone above the desired Fm7. The melodic line begins on an A natural – the 3rd of F#m7 – and as the left hand chord moves down to Fm7, the melody descends chromatically. In bar 2 the line emphasises both the b9 and #9 of Bb7. Thereafter it takes on a decidedly bebop shape and could easily be a Bud Powell phrase if not for the Corea-style staccato articulation.

Example 8f

Example 8g is our only Chick lick in 3/4 time. He often explores three time and his tune *Windows* which has become a standard is a good example. We are back to a single chord vamp for this idea and the lines come from G Mixolydian. Corea often punctuates his solos with pithy licks such as this. Here the melodic line is sliding between fourths, with each fourth taken down a step to form a descending pattern. Played Corea-style the effect is a flamenco-like flourish.

Example 8g

The next lick takes a similar approach to the previous one in its execution. This time the tonal centre is F Mixolydian and the short melodic motif descends each time it is played. It moves down a whole step each time, which means that it moves outside the harmony. Instead of the sliding effect used previously, here there is a clear separation between the notes. This lick needs to be played with percussive energy – not a heavy touch, but with rhythmic precision. Corea played the drums when he was growing up and this precise, percussive aspect can be heard in the execution.

Example 8h

For example 8i we move to minor ii V I in C minor. Notice the repeated G note in bar 2 before the line jumps up a fourth to play an Ab (b9 of G7) and Db (#11). These altered tensions are the climax of the lick, before it descends, the melodic line becoming chromatic in bar 3. It eventually settles on a Cm11. Ending on a big chord is something Corea is fond of doing and executes very effectively.

Example 8i

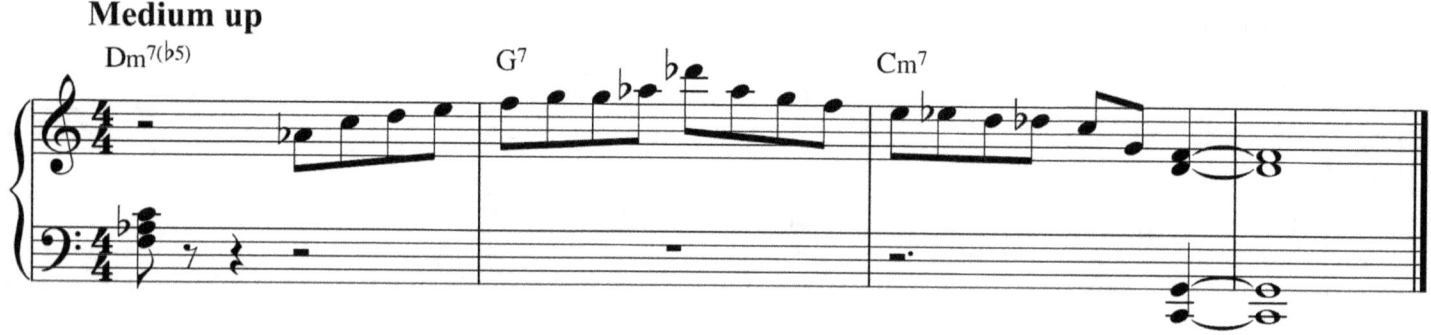

Chick Corea played a lot music that fused jazz and Latin American styles. In this final lick we see some of his Latin influence coming through. The lick opens with a *montuno* figure. This originates from Cuban music and essentially describes a syncopated piano vamp. The figure descends using a mixture of octave jumps and the chromatic scale and culminates in a big Gm7 chord.

Chromaticism, large intervals mixed with quartal voicings, and an unmistakable Latin influence – all these contribute to the broad, yet very recognisable style of the great Chick Corea.

Example 8j

9. Keith Jarrett

It is difficult not to think of Keith Jarrett as a freak of nature! "Phenomenon" is a word that springs to mind. The man's seemingly limitless technical abilities on the piano are matched only by his seemingly endless store of *seriously musical* ideas. His ability to produce pretty much whatever he wants on the piano at any given moment means that his improvisation is so pure, it's difficult to conceive of such a thing as a "Keith Jarrett lick". More on that in a moment.

Keith Jarrett was born on May 8, 1945, in Allentown, Pennsylvania. He started playing piano at a very early age (2 or 3) and it was soon clear that he was a precocious talent. He began performing the classical repertoire as well as his own compositions at the age of seven. Even as a young child he wanted to alter some of the notes in the great classics that he was learning – an early indication of his creative mind and the future path he would take.

As a teenager he was offered a golden opportunity to study classical piano in Paris with Nadia Boulanger, but by this time he had discovered jazz music and the creative freedom it affords. Instead, he went to New York in 1964 to pursue his career. Here he frequented the Village Vanguard jam session in an effort to be heard by some of the jazz greats who were often in attendance. Jarrett's shyness and inability to push himself forward meant that he spent many visits as a spectator, but his persistence paid dividend in the end. One night when he got the chance to play, the great Art Blakey heard him and Jarrett soon found himself touring with the legendary Jazz Messengers and made his debut recording with them.

George Coleman was the next bandleader to recognise the young pianist's talent. In 1966 Jarrett toured with the extremely popular George Coleman Quartet and was with them for two years. It was in this band that he first worked with drummer Jack DeJohnette, forming what has proved to be a lifelong and significant working relationship for both musicians.

In the late 1960s, Jarrett began making albums under his own name. He formed a trio consisting of ex Bill Evans drummer Paul Motian (a master of both space and time) and bass innovator of the Ornette Coleman band, Charlie Haden. The trio played a wide range of material from free improvisation and Ornette Coleman-esque "time no changes", to florid rubato ballads laid alongside relatively straight ahead jazz. Jarrett made use of many different styles and grooves, writing pieces with distinctive folk, pop or rock sounds as well as more orthodox jazz, but always acoustic and always exquisitely designed. The trio was later to be joined by saxophonist Dewey Redman and became known as Jarrett's "American quartet".

In 1970 Miles Davis came calling and Jarrett agreed to join his band. He had the unique experience of working with another keyboardist in the same group – the great Chick Corea. In later life, he and Chick Corea teamed up in very different circumstances to play a Mozart double piano concerto! Jarrett dislikes playing electronic instruments, but made an exception for Miles Davis. Significantly, Jack DeJohnette was also in Miles' band during that period.

In 1971, Jarrett met the founder of the European recording company ECM, Manfred Eicher. A long and fruitful partnership began between the two men which continues to this day. Eicher gave Jarrett artistic freedom coupled with impeccable production quality and Jarrett has given Eicher many beautiful albums including the famous, *The Köln Concert*.

The Köln Concert was recorded in 1975 and was Jarrett's 6th album for ECM. It remains not only his most bought album but the highest selling solo piano album of any style ever, shifting over 3.5 million copies! The concept was simple: Jarrett went on a tour of concert halls and opera houses giving totally improvised solo piano performances. On this occasion the concert was booked for 11:30pm and Jarrett (who hadn't slept for several days) arrived to find that the piano he had requested was not on the stage. Instead, there was a tinny sounding baby grand. There had been a mistake among the staff of the opera house and there was no time to rectify it. Jarrett refused to play at first, but was talked round by the concert organiser/promoter Vera Brandes who was (incredibly) only 17 years old at the time. Jarrett was forced to play in a certain way to get the most out of the piano and opted for repetitive bass grooves and fairly simple harmonic structures. The result is an accessible masterpiece through which millions have enjoyed the unprecedented artistry of Keith Jarrett.

As well as the solo performances and recordings, Eicher facilitated a project with Norwegian saxophonist Jan Garbarek. Jarrett's so called "European quartet" featured Garbarek on saxophones, Palle Danielsson on double bass and Jon Christensen on drums. It ran concurrently with his American quartet for a time and continued after it. The band produced some of the most beautiful music of the seventies and helped to define the sound of European jazz/improvised music. Some of Jarrett's most beguiling writing and stunning performances were captured in this band. Check out the albums *My Song* and *Personal Mountains*.

In January 1983, Jarrett recorded a trio album. In fact, the trio recorded enough material to make three albums in under three days. Eicher had suggested Jarrett team up with bassist Gary Peacock (a Bill Evans trio alumnus) and his old colleague Jack DeJohnette (also an Evans veteran). The trio decided to record mostly standards, doing what thousands of jazz musicians around the world do every day: interpret and improvise over the great shared repertoire. The albums were a great success and the trio has become known as "the standards trio". This group is one of the longest running jazz trios ever, finally disbanding in 2014. They have left a substantial discography, all of it improvised jazz of the absolute highest quality. The *Blue Note Sessions* and *At the Dear Head Inn* (Paul Motian replaces DeJohnette for this one) are my personal favourites.

Jarrett has also recorded a large amount of classical music and written his own beautiful orchestral music. Whatever he does, he gives 100% commitment to. "It's the whole nine yards." he once said in an interview. When he improvises, his body dances and writhes as he plays – rarely does he settle on the piano stool – and he vocalises his ideas, singing them as if there's too much music in him for just the piano to handle.

Keith Jarrett's music is a must for any pianist, regardless of style. Be warned though, you could get seriously hooked!

Keith Jarrett's style

As mentioned in the introduction to this chapter, Keith Jarrett is a pure improviser and, as such, you can't really understand his style in lick form. We can learn more by studying his approach as a whole, and below is a 58-bar solo (much more than 10 licks' worth!) which we will analyse.

The use of space and context are very important things to notice in Jarrett's playing. What he chooses to play always relates to what he has just played and informs what he will play next. His melodic ideas form a wider arc and create a narrative for the entire solo.

This Jarrett-style solo is played over a looping ii V iii vi progression in the key of F Major. Jarrett has used this circular vamp as an outro on a number of recordings, following a Miles Davis tradition. It's the kind of thing you'll hear Jarrett do in his Standards Trio recordings.

Analysis

Taking an overview of the solo, notice that there is plenty of space – especially in the left hand. Though Jarrett's left hand is capable of virtuosic feats beyond most pianists (listen to his solo recordings) he often restricts himself to short, sparse accompaniment in a band setting to allow his singing right hand melodic ideas full reign. To begin with, the right hand is also sparse – the ideas build in intensity slowly, with more notes later on. Leaving chunks of space is all part of the process.

The solo begins with simple phrases using mostly diatonic notes. In the first phrase, the tonal centre is highlighted with an F note that is repeated an octave lower. The phrase ends in bar 3 with a jump of a seventh. The next motif (bars 5-6) picks up on the idea of sevenths. The tonal centre is asserted again at the end of bar 8 with an F note, but instead of repeating it down an octave, this time the "blue" note of Ab is introduced and emphasised with octaves.

By the time we reach bars 12-14 we encounter an idea that occurred in bar 2, though this time it's played over different chords. This illustrates how Jarrett never loses sight of his melodic narrative – nothing is simply a random lick. So far, the solo has an ageless quality – it could have been played by Louis Armstrong or a 1950s Miles Davis. There is always a deep sense of jazz history in Jarrett's playing, which is particularly noticeable in his trio recordings.

A more chromatic bebop flavour creeps in around bars 16-18, but the lyrical aesthetic of the melody is still present. The descending motif which closes the phrase in bar 18 becomes the catalyst for the next string of ideas (bars 20-25) which culminate in an ascending pattern using altered notes over the D7 chord: Eb (b9), F (#9) and G# (#11). The triplet flourish in bars 26-27 mimics the ending of the previously stated altered lick.

The intensity of the solo has risen and once again the tonal centre is stated in octaves. This short, assertive phrase is followed by some unexpected space, which actually serves to ramp up the tension. The release finally comes in bar 32 with a restatement of the F octaves that leads into a long bebop line that ends in bar 37. This ushers in a more intense use of octaves and chromaticism. The descending chromatic octave figure subtly references the rhythm used in bars 23-24.

Bar 46 highlights the kind of technical prowess Jarrett is capable of, with a line that begins with triplets and morphs into 1/16 notes. There are two things to notice here: one, that Jarrett will only execute an impressive line like this as the occasion demands, and two: even when playing a long 1/16 note run, Jarrett won't resort to a predictable run. Instead, the lines mixes and matches a couple of motifs in a non-predictable but entirely coherent way. The phrase closes beautifully in bar 49.

The solo returns to the simpler melodic language of the first sixteen bars to bring it down for a comfortable landing to finish.

Example 9a

58

10. Brad Mehldau

Brad Mehldau is undoubtedly the most original and distinctive voice to emerge from his generation of jazz musicians. In these days, when everybody seems to be trying to do something original, he has managed to achieve a truly unique sound. He is a musician with a strong stylistic concept crafted and honed over thousands of solitary hours at the keyboard. His innovations lie not in outlandish stunts or novel instrumentation, but within the confines of the traditional jazz piano trio. Much of his unique sound is achieved through his approach to texture. He has unlocked the possibilities to be found in counterpoint, using the left hand to play melodic lines as well as the right, and pulling off flawless improvised contrapuntal passages that leaves the listener breathless. He also has an empirical mastery of harmony, allowing melodic motifs to wander their own way, becoming seemingly detached from the chords, but following a strong internal logic. His technical capabilities seem to defy nature!

Born in Jacksonville, Florida, in 1970, Brad Mehldau had a pretty stable family life. His father was a doctor and mother a homemaker. He began piano lessons at the age of six and acquired a love for classical music as well as a solid piano technique.

In his early teens he discovered jazz through an Oscar Peterson record bought for him by a family friend. Mehldau was impressed by Peterson's technical prowess and the music chimed with his love for improvisation. More investigation followed and he was greatly affected by the Keith Jarrett solo record *Bremen/Lausanne*. Mehldau began to immerse himself in the music of the great jazz musicians, studying, transcribing and imbibing the sounds.

Mehldau played in his high school jazz band which was good enough to do regular gigs. He won the notable prize of "Best all round musician award for school students" presented by the Berklee College of Music. He moved to New York city to study jazz in 1988. Among his teachers were jazz luminary pianists such as Kenny Werner and Fred Hersch. The drummer Jimmy Cobb of Miles Davis *Kind of Blue* fame was also on the faculty. Cobb employed the young pianist for his band Cobb's Mob and the early nineties saw Mehldau's reputation grow.

Mehldau made his mark on the international scene when he joined the Joshua Redman Quartet. This band was a supergroup of the young jazz talent on offer at the time. In addition to Redman on sax and Mehldau on piano, Christian McBride was on double bass and Brian Blade on drums. All four musicians have remained in the top flight of the jazz world ever since.

Around this time Mehldau formed a trio with bass player Larry Grenadier and drummer Jorge Rossy. Mehldau and Rossy would have practice sessions where they played standards and put them into odd time signatures, like 5/4 or 7/4. Their aim was to become as comfortable playing in 7/4 time as they were in 4/4. Mehldau's extensive use of odd time signatures on standard tunes became something of a trademark.

Mehldau's style was developing. In his younger days he would play like Wynton Kelly or McCoy Tyner as the occasion demanded, but a new and more distinctive sound was emerging. His articulation became crisp, clipped and almost over-intentional at times. At the peak of his solos, sometimes his right hand would play ostinato-like arpeggios, while his left hand took on the melodic role. His love of German romantic classical music came to the fore in his original compositions, sometimes using very classical sounding broken chord accompaniment in his left hand. As well as this classical influence, Mehldau would take music from the contemporary mainstream and give it the jazz treatment using songs by Radiohead, Paul Simon and others in his regular set. Jazz fans of the time, hungry for new sounds, devoured his trio albums and Mehldau became the next great pianist to move jazz piano onward.

Mehldau has made many albums including partnerships with guitarist Pat Metheny and mandolinist extraordinaire Chris Theale among notable others. He has written music for large scale ensembles as well as solo piano pieces, often blurring the lines of genres. He has always (at least until now) returned to the piano trio context, finding new sounds and further developing his concept and musical language. His contrapuntal playing is becoming ever more sophisticated: from those early recordings, with the right hand ostinato figures and simple left hand melodic fragments, to the present day with a complex interplay between multiple melodic lines.

Mehldau remains at the forefront of jazz innovation and with his career still unfolding, it is an exciting prospect to follow his progress and hear his latest recordings.

Brad Mehldau's style

Mehldau is known for his precise execution, immaculate technique and sophisticated manipulation of harmony. Give the latter, his playing contains a surprising amount of blues language, and this is evident in the first example lick. Played over an G7 chord to a straight groove, it has a slightly rock/funk feel. A little pick-up motif in the right hand sets us up for the main body of the lick which is played with the left hand. Mehldau often uses his left hand to play melodic lines – something that was hardly ever done before he appeared on the scene.

The notes in bar 1 outline a G major arpeggio, but in bar 2 a variation of the melodic pattern is played down a tone, suggesting F major. The lick lands on a B note (3rd of G7) and G notes an octave apart at the end to resolve the lick to G7. This kind of melodic digression is common in Mehldau's style.

Example 10a

In the second example, the left hand is heavily employed again. The right hand begins the idea, then relinquishes the role to the left. In this example, the right hand continues playing, but takes an accompanying role. Repeated notes play a large role in Mehldau's music. Here we have a repeating Ab that hammers home the bluesy element of the lick. The left hand imitates the melody then develops it further with chromatic and bluesy-sounding language: a G# is jammed alongside an A natural and held – it's not just a passing note. The result is a slightly jarring type of blues.

Example 10b

Example 10c has a more traditional division of labour between the hands. The left hand plays a chord and the right hand does the rest. The harmony is based on a Gsus chord and the melodic line begins with a short chromatic run that shifts up a minor third and down again, ending on a C#. This opening motif creates the feeling that the phrase is floating above, slightly detached from the harmony.

Bar 2 begins with the suggestion that we might be settling into our G major harmony, but then dives into a Bb major arpeggio. A chromatic passing note takes us into the last bar which contains a conventional sounding G major bluesy motif, which at last brings us in line with the chord.

Example 10c

Example 10d has the left hand playing one chord per bar, switching between Ebsus and Dbsus. The groove is a slow 3/4 time swing, but the notes played in the right hand are mostly 1/16ths and dotted 1/8th notes. The melodic line begins with a #9 note, enforcing a bluesy sound in a bullish, slightly forced way. The line then meanders in a different direction to the harmony, but retains its own strong internal logic. In bar 2 an A major arpeggio is used as the first point of departure (A is the b5 or tritone of Eb). In bar 3 the A major shape moves into a D major shape – a perfect cadence in D. This idea continues until the lick finds its way back to Eb major, finishing with the note Eb repeated in triplets, as if to reinforce the 3/4 time signature.

Example 10d

In this lick we start to explore one of the trademark sounds of Mehldau's early years. The right hand is playing an arpeggiated ostinato type figure to create a high textural layer. It forms a dynamic accompaniment to any melodies played by the left hand. In this case we have a simple little phrase that could have been played by anyone. What makes it special and typical of Mehldau is the fact that it's played in the left hand, and in the context of that glistening right hand pattern.

Example 10e

Example 10f contains elements of all the licks so far. The right hand melodic line is somewhat detached from the harmony but follows its own logic. It descends in major thirds, an E major shape flowing into a C major shape, which flows into an Ab major shape. The left hand begins with a chord, but then plays a short counter melody causing an effect similar to the previous example. This time the lick is more truly contrapuntal with both hands offering melodic phrases. Mehldau is fond of making counter melodies emerge from the middle of the texture, while the right hand line is still blazing away. It's a pretty stunning trick if you can do it!

Example 10f

Example 10g has more counterpoint, this time led by the left hand. The tonal centre is F minor. The left hand kicks things off with a bebop sounding chromatic run that descends from E natural to C, then into an F minor arpeggio. This first motif sets up an FmMaj7 sound. This idea is taken up by the right hand which also plays the E natural, an Fm7 arpeggio, and finishes by jamming together Eb (minor 7th) and E (major 7th) notes.

In bar 2 the left hand continues with the "chromatic line into an arpeggio" idea. In turn, the right hand develops the unsettling chromatic "crush" of clashing major and minor sevenths. The transition from bar 3 to 4 has the left hand playing a similar shape, but displacing it. Like most modern jazz pianists, Mehldau is very fond of using rhythmic displacement to free up the phrasing. The right hand continues with the crushed notes but further up the piano. The overall effect is that the hands follow each in a type of contrary motion throughout the lick.

Example 10g

In this lick we take a look at Mehldau's more romantic side. Mehldau makes no secret of his love for German romantic piano music, counting Brahms and Schumann among his musical influences. The left hand activity gives the biggest hint of these influences, laying down a proper standalone accompaniment instead of just chords or a contrapuntal melodic role. The bass note gradually descends chromatically as the chords interject rhythmically. The chords are arranged in a more classical way, using inversions – such as Ab/Eb and Bb/D in bar 2.

The harmonic sequence captures the passionate ascetic of Brahms or Schumann – a far cry from the 12-bar blues! The melody line in the right hand is harmonically orthodox but asserts a rhythmic freedom by the use of triplets and ties in bar 1, straight 1/8 notes against the swing rhythm in bar 2, and quadruplet 1/4 notes in bar 3. The repeated C notes in bar 2 are typical of Mehldau and this, coupled with the fact that this excerpt is in the odd time of signature of 5/4, is the only indication that this piece is modern and doesn't originate from the late 1800s.

Example 10h

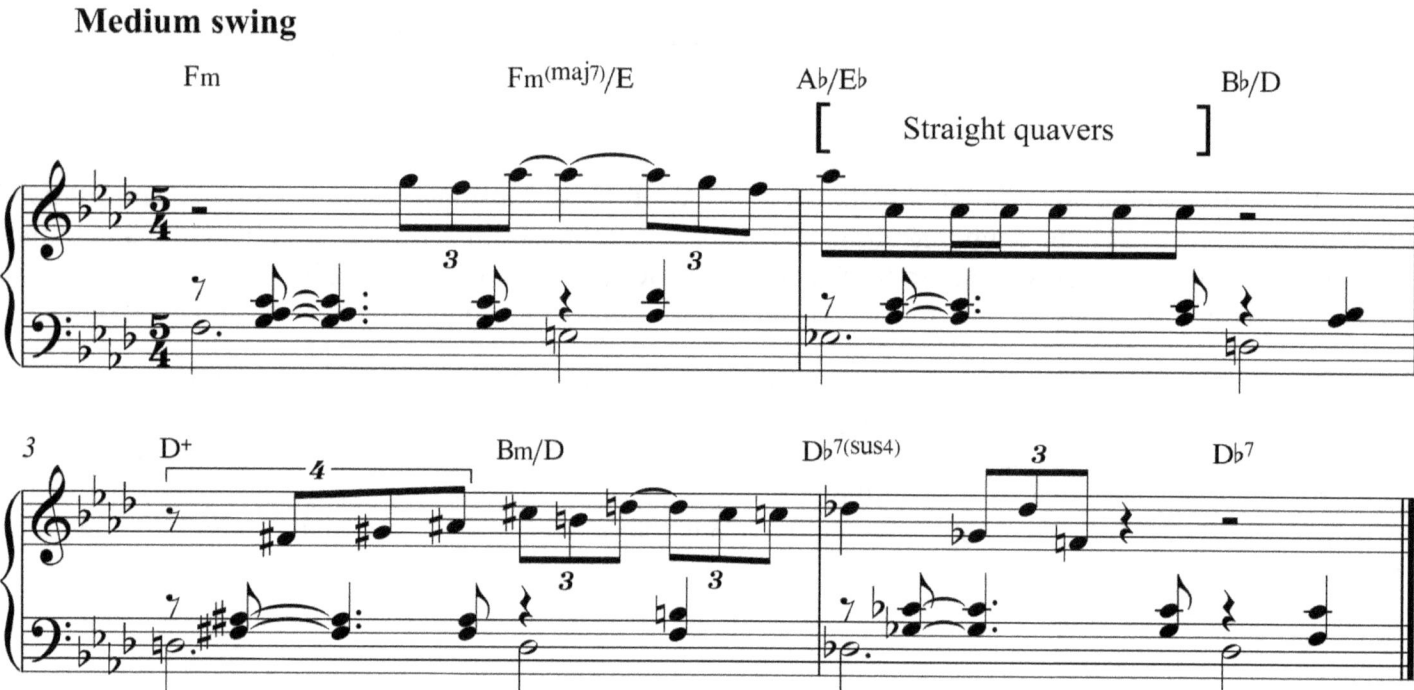

In the previous lick we introduced the odd time signature of 5/4. The next two are in 7/4 time. It's impossible to write ten licks in the style of Brad Mehldau and *not* include some in these less common time signatures. If you are not so used to playing in seven, then listen to the lick lots of time before you play it, and seek out some other tunes in 7/4 to listen to.

To count in 7/4, *don't* count to seven, but divide the bar like this:

One, two, three, four, one, two, three… *one,* two, three, four, one, two, three…

In this example, the right hand plays its traditional melodic role while the left hand holds down a very open voicing of Cmaj7. The ambiguous voicing allows the right hand to wander through different tonal centres (E, C, Ab and then C Major). Chromaticism coupled with triadic shapes is typical Mehldau.

Example 10i

For the last lick of this book it seems appropriate to leave you with a challenge! Brad Mehldau's concept of harmony and his technical skills have reached such a peak of development that he can improvise with both hands at once in odd time signatures, and at practically any tempo. For this lick I've written a chord sequence to work over.

In the right hand we have a more developed version of the ostinato idea we explored in Example 10e. This time the ostinato is not static but varies. This variation is not just to adapt to the chord changes, as you might expect, but the top notes create their own overarching melodic line.

The left hand takes on the main voice in this lick, After dropping briefly from C to Ab to emphasise the first chord change, the line rises using bebop chromatic passing notes and an Ab major arpeggio. It peaks at Eb on beat 3 of bar 2, then descends using some blue notes to lead us back to an F Major finish.

Once again, my advice is to listen to the lick multiple times so that you know it thoroughly in your head before you attempt to play it. In addition, this time you might want to learn each hand separately first. Learn it slowly and give yourself a chance. Enjoy!

Example 10j

Up swing

Conclusion

I hope you've enjoyed this journey into the styles of ten of the greats of jazz piano. I trust that the short biographies have given you an insight into the musical heritage of each player (it's helpful to know what previous music has informed their own), and I hope the discussion of the harmonic/melodic devices used by each player is a creative springboard to explore your own ideas.

I've included references to albums throughout this book, but check out as much music as you can from each player as you learn the licks. It will help you to understand *why* they play in a certain way, and you'll also discover how their music developed over time.

Remember, it's one thing to be able to regurgitate a phrase or two, but another thing entirely to speak a language fluently. Treat this book like a phrasebook you can keep referring to while you're learning to speak the language of modern jazz piano fluently.

Enjoy your playing!

Nathan.

www.ingramcontent.com/pod-product-compliance
Lightning Source LLC
LaVergne TN
LVHW061255060426
835507LV00020B/2326